IN DETAIL | **BARCELONA CONTEMPORARY ARCHITECTURE**

Quim Larrea

IN DETAIL | BARCELONA CONTEMPORARY ARCHITECTURE

Photographs by Alejo Bagué, Lluís Casals, Lurdes Jansana,
Duccio Malagamba, Pepe Navarro, Eugeni Pons, Xavier Ribas,
Hisao Suzuki and Rafael Vargas

Ediciones Polígrafa

© 2005 Ediciones Polígrafa, S. A.
Balmes, 54 - 08007 Barcelona
www.edicionespoligrafa.com

Texts ©: Quim Larrea
Photographs ©: The named photographers
(except: J. Orpinell, pp. 62-63; Sergio Belinchón, p. 64 ; Kristien Daem, pp. 74-75)
Translation: Sue Brownbridge
Coordination: Montse Holgado
Design: Estudio Polígrafa / B. Martínez
Copy editing: Rafael Galisteo, Sue Brownbridge

I.S.B.N.: 84–343–1090–2
D.L.: B. 36.773 – 2005 (Printed in Spain)

Color Separation: Format Digital, Barcelona
Printing and binding: Mateo Cromo, Madrid

Available in the USA and Canada through D.A.P. / Distributed Art Publishers.
155 Sixth Avenue, 2nd Floor, New York, N.Y. 10013 – Tel.: (212) 627–9484

CONTENTS

Like icons arranged on the surface of the planet, cities orientate the land. Travelers set out from and make their way to cities. The city is in itself the referent, the beacon indicating the way and making the cultural and geographic situation possible, the place of encounter where relationships are established and information shared.[1]

Contradictorily human, the city has adopted numerous approaches, all of them ambiguous, all of them hybrid, all of them in the throes of constant transformation.

Barcelona follows one of these approaches that we subjectively recognize as Mediterranean.

The city's situation on the seashore and its Latin foundation are decisive contributory factors in this labeling. In addition, however, to the characteristics that are testimony of its geographical location or its past is the clear organization of its urban fabric—which is closely bound up with its history—in which the center is easily recognizable. This center continues to act in an evident manner on the rest of the city, the old neighboring towns that have retained their own character and the Eixample, that vast unifying swathe that occupies the territory and binds and compacts it.

The Mediterranean city has forged a special relationship between the private space and the public space—as a result of the uses they are put to by residents in accordance with their needs—the organization of the avenues and their hierarchy, the location of squares, which are essential and that act as magnets, attracting to themselves the life of the city, and the importance of open spaces, an ambiguous term for something traditionally known as parks and gardens.

A study of the lie of the land of Barcelona soon reveals it to be a plain hemmed in by the natural boundaries around it: two rivers, the sea, the slopes of the massif of Montjuïc and the Collserola chain of hills. In short, this is a finite territory that has been urbanized and built up.

Buildings of a reasonable height have been erected on this land, producing a unified effect that is broken solely by certain edifices that stand out due to their social or monumental function or because of their strategic location.

A good combination of residential accommodation and services of varying size and density, sufficiently well distributed across the territory, has given the city the compactness so forcefully advocated and so strongly approved of by Oriol Bohigas.[2]

Barcelona is like a multi-layered gateau placed on the territory. Or rather, it is like a thick pile carpet that molds itself gently to the contours of the land, covering the entire plain and spreading up the slopes towards the hilltops, where it frays into a fringed edge, or down towards the shoreline, where it is neatly trimmed.[3]

The Eixample, designed by Ildefons Cerdà, is responsible for the look of Barcelona. Rather than simply turning a valley of market gardens and orchards into a city, Cerdà essentially designed a rigid grid—a classic feature of the Mediterranean city, whose references go much further back than the Cardus Maximus or Decumanus Maximus of the Romans to the cities founded before Ptolemy in ancient Egypt—to which he added features that brought it soberly into the modern era, the chamfered street corners, diagonal boulevards and wide avenues crisscrossing at right angles, and the nearby park. Nowadays, a century and a half after it was designed, the Eixample remains efficient and has coped with all kinds of change: the filling-in of the four facades of the street blocks so that no gaps are left; the impact of and the link with the urban fabric of other population centers in the plain; the occupation of the inner courtyards and the increased height of buildings; the appearance of motorized vehicles and their appropriation of the highway; the creation of industrial sectors; the various subway lines; the successive enhancements to buildings and the excrescences of attics and the additional floors built above them in the 1970s; bus and taxi lanes and bike lanes; and even the blue and green parking zones for outsiders and local residents. The Eixample is, in short, an urban jewel that has become the emblem of the city and a much-envied form of heritage that can be neither repeated nor, fortunately, squandered.

Unsurprisingly, Cerdà's plan was not immediately implemented. As more land was required by the city, the grid expanded to provide it. In general, this land was for mixed residential and tertiary use, though pockets where industry happily took root did form.

By the end of the 20th century, the entire area that had once been a valley of orchards, market gardens and mountain streams was occupied by the metropolis, all except, that is, a last redoubt in the northern part of the city at the delta where the mouth of the Besòs River meets the sea.

This was "the last pocket of land in Barcelona,"[4] a final stronghold of just over 34 hectares at the end of the Avinguda Diagonal boulevard that crosses Barcelona. It is here that the Diagonal Mar development and the complexes erected for the Forum of Cultures, the first major event held in Barcelona in the 21st century, have taken shape. The Forum not only constituted an opportune force driving the transformation and urbanization of this area of the city, but also bequeathed Barcelona a number of amenities—some of them new and others relocated from elsewhere—that have indisputably marked a turning point in the city and ushered in a new future.

These amenities and buildings include tower blocks over 300 hundred feet tall—such as the AC Hotel, Princess Diagonal, Illa del Mar, Illa del Llac and office blocks in Zona Franca—the Plaça de la Pau, the second largest such plaza in the world, a congress center with a capacity for up to 15,000 people, hotels, beach areas, a new pleasure harbor, a huge pergola covered in solar devices, etc.

All of this is on a vast scale beyond anything the city had known before. This is an area in which gigantism has established itself, forging a relationship—though one that is difficult to read—with the pre-existing buildings and urban fabric, the coast and the features on either bank of the Besòs River.

The rules of the game have changed in the compact, homogenous carpet that the city of Barcelona once was. In Plaça del les Glòries, we find Nouvel's intervention of the Agbar Tower, rising more than 450 feet in height, followed by the Ona Building, designed by Federico Soriano and Dolores Palacios for Barcelona City Hall, a new building by the English architect David Chipperfield and an area of six new office blocks. This selfsame district will also be home to the building that will house the city's new design museum, the work of the Martorell-Bohigas-Mackay studio. These constructions, together with the Hotel Silken by Juli Capella, the existing shopping center and the refurbishment of the La Farinera building will unquestionably make this area a major draw in the city, though it is open to question whether it will ever be the focal point that Ildefons Cerdà dreamed of a century and a half ago.

All of this has taken place on the fringes of the new 22@ district, which was brought into being with the intention of transforming a largely industrial area into a services district and fashioning it into a link with the neighborhoods to the northeast of the city and the Vila Olímpica.

Four new tower blocks have also been built along the shoreline.

The construction of towers on the shore is not a new phenomenon. The twin buildings alongside the Vila Olímpica port are an obvious and nearby precedent and indeed the original plan for this residential area—drawn up by MBM Architects—included six towers, though the Ministry of Public Works' scissors made short work of them during a trip to Madrid.[5]

Frank Gehry has designed the nearly 500-foot-high Torre del Triangle Ferroviari, which is due to be completed in the Sagrera district in 2007, and that will serve as the setting for the arrival of the long-awaited high-speed train

The Agbar Tower is barely a taster of what is to come in Barcelona, with the construction of the Hotel Vela by Ricardo Bofill, the offices in Zona Franca, the Torre del Gas by Miralles and Tagliabue, the Habitat Sky—375 feet tall—by Perrault and the Fira towers by Toyo Ito on the other side of Montjuïc.[6]

Barcelona has indisputably embraced tall buildings.

The appearance of these towers has initiated the engaging debate on skyscrapers and prompted a comparison with the American city model, though this is somewhat naïve given that from an international perspective Barcelona is a small city in terms of the number of its residents and its economic importance.

The first skyscrapers went up in the United States towards the close of the 19th century. There can be no doubt that they have shaped numerous American cities, with their promoters' ego or the pursuit of ostentation[7] prevailing over urban suitability or efficient functionality.

The idea of tall buildings inevitably brings us to the concept of the "skyline," the silhouette of a city as it breaks through the horizon. If we were called upon to say what the Barcelona skyline is, we would undoubtedly have to accept that it is made up of the profile of the Collserola chain of hills, with the eye-catching church on Mount Tibidabo (at an altitude of approximately 1700 feet and hence much higher than any building that will ever be built in the city) and the magnificent Communications Tower designed by Norman Foster. This privileged spot combines modernity, technology, history and respect for nature. Nor should we forget the fact that Collserola is the city's vast urban park. In addition, this skyline is not only visible from the coast but also reminds towns inland of Barcelona's presence.

In the last 15 years, Barcelona has acquired two new districts. A third is now being finalized and a fourth is being planned on the outskirts in Zona Franca by the architects Alejandro Zaera and Arata Isozaki. Nevertheless, it is difficult to perceive the model that governs these actions, and even though the slogans in the Bohigas style, foremost among them "let's monumentalize the periphery", continue to bear fruit, one feels the lack of any theoretical machinery behind the new drive for development and growth in the city.

At this stage, we should be turning our attention back to the venerable Eixample and analyzing whether it is able to respond to the new challenges because sooner or later we will need to commit ourselves to further work in the district.

If we take as our reference the type of city being planned in the new neighborhoods and the importance that tall buildings are acquiring in them, it becomes evident that there is every reason why we should be considering this kind of intervention in the Eixample as well. After all, two blocks in the grid design proposed by Cerdà cover a greater surface area than a single block in Manhattan,[8] so it would be possible to instigate a conceptual urban unity—while respecting the road layout—of the "double block" that could easily bear the construction of a building 300 feet and more tall. The plot required—around 11,000 square feet—would not seem unduly excessive in relation to the more than 215,000 square feet of surface area of this new unit.

These tower blocks could be put to mixed residential and office use, with retail outlets on the ground floor, a tried and tested formula that has been shown to be effective.

The municipality's experienced urban development team could professionally structure the necessary compensations and adjustments. After all, this was done 150 years ago when farmland was turned into streets and building plots.

This would make it possible to "re-compact" most of the plain, to stimulate small retail businesses, to provide new housing in the heart of the city and, with the appropriate compensation, to reclaim the inner courtyards in street blocks as public spaces—thereby fulfilling a long-held desire among citizens—with underground car parks below them.

All of this could be achieved by exploiting existing infrastructure and would not take any toll on it. Perhaps the most decisive factor is that there would be no need to find new building land, a resource that is particularly scarce in Barcelona.

The formal result would be the appearance in the carpet of Barcelona of a series of needles strategically and homogenously situated across the territory, producing a new image of the Eixample.

The quality of the architecture in this new compacting of Barcelona would give rise to competition between leading Spanish and international architects, something the city is already used to.

In the last 20 years, and particularly recently, distinguished architects from around the world have been invited to produce designs for the city in direct collaboration with local studios, which have been able to contribute their local knowledge and sensibility to projects dreamt up on drawing boards in places far from the locations that the works were intended for.

It would seem that the city is consumed with a passion for collecting and that what started out as an international contribution to the Olympic facilities, financed by public capital, has become a mark of status in buildings and has prompted private initiative to invest as well.

A new tendency, a neo-monumentalism, holds sway at the moment: it is no longer enough for a building to be striking, as the signature of its artificer is now of supreme importance. This effect is very far from being local and nowadays any city with a sense of pride numbers works by eminent architects among its emblematic buildings or those in the pipeline. A scant 200 studios, a number of them Spanish and some of them based in Barcelona, sow their works around the entire world. One only has to visit these practices to discover the projects in progress across the globe in Beijing, San Francisco, Mexico, New York, Sidney and elsewhere.

Works leap from city to city, country to country and even from continent to continent with surprising facility, to the extent that it is difficult to recall with instant certainty whether a particular building stands in Hudson Bay or on the estuary of the city of Bilbao. New buildings such as these rejuvenate the architectural heritage of the city and vie for attention, competing not only with each other but with monumental buildings from the past—as evidenced by the fact that every major city includes a guide to its architecture among its range of attractions for tourists—all the while tending to form theme parks for the *cognoscenti*. Perhaps what we have here is something that we might easily term "International Monumentalism," a new global style in which the resolution of the dichotomy of "form and function" is neither all-prevailing nor even sufficient and to which a third category needs to be added, that of the "author."

The only possible response to this situation is questioning and reflection. If author is equal to brand, and if the brand is the leitmotiv of marketing, and if the purpose of marketing is to sell, we might reasonably ask ourselves whether it is the best architecture that is being built or that which was sold best. A sensible answer to this doubt is to be found in the work of Glenn Murcutt, the recent Pritzker Prize Laureate[9] and an admirer of the work of José Antonio Coderch, or in the words of Ignasi de Solà-Morales: "These brilliant, seductive, attractive buildings usually declare much more about the city than their authors apparently say. Theirs is, if you will, a subliminal, non-explicit message and hence they favor a city of singular objects, a city full of emotional outbursts lost among the gray magma of ordinary output. The city would find it difficult to bear the concentration of sublime experiences, and both time and changes in taste are busy giving ephemeral life to these beacons of aesthetic stimulation charged with powerful hedonistic messages. Yet in them, there is an idea of a city related to the individualism typical of our culture, to the competitive struggle to take the lead and to draw all the attention. The city of stellar buildings is the city of VIPs, of stars, of the Forbes rankings or Guinness records, of the fierce tussle in the marketplace between all kinds of products."[10]

Notes

1. "The city is usually the physical and social place where the greatest—perhaps the best—possibilities for sharing information, communication and the immediate supply of this information occur." Oriol Bohigas: *Contra la incontinència urbana. Reconsideració moral de l'arquitectura i la ciutat.* Institut d'Edicions de la Diputació de Barcelona, Barcelona, 2004.

2. Oriol Bohigas, op. cit.

3. Elías Torres and José Antonio Martínez Lapeña gave this interpretation in a rug made in La Alpujarra in 1986 and produced by BD Ediciones de Diseño.

4. "The city is going through a second rejuvenation, which is concentrated in Poblenou and the district of Sant Martí, the last pocket of land left in Barcelona." Interview with Lee Mays, Managing Director of Diagonal Mar, published in *La Vanguardia,* 21 October 2001.

5. "The ministry in Madrid organized an exhibition showing progress on the projects for the Olympic Games. There was a model of the Vila Olímpica with six towers. On the eve of the opening, a very progressive director general went through the exhibition and very rashly ripped up the six towers with his own hands in horror at the bad example set at a time when it was being proposed that the coastline should be swept clean of the horrendous buildings spoiling it." Oriol Bohigas: *Contra la incontinència urbana. Reconsideració moral de l'arquitectura i la ciutat.* Institut d'Edicions de la Diputació de Barcelona, Barcelona, 2004.

6. The timid antecedents for these tall buildings date back to the time of the mayor Josep Maria de Porcioles, who allowed the Torre Colón in the Raval, the Banco Atlántico building on the corner of the junction between Avinguda Diagonal and Balmes, the Atalaya building and the Torre Urquinaona, all buildings that stand out above the skyline, interrupting the panoramic view across the city and out to sea from Tibidabo.

7. The paradigmatic skyscraper is the Empire State Building—perhaps too obvious an example—which was built in 1929. It is three times the height of the Agbar Tower—at 1454 feet including the lightning conductor—and is well-known to everyone as one of the emblems of the city of New York.

8. The 1811 Commissioners Plan established the New York block as 200 by 920 feet—around 4.2 acres—while two blocks in the Eixample measures 371 by just over 738 feet, or 6.2 hectares.

9. *"The architecture in vogue today is now close to sculpture."*
"I'm not interested in sculptural architecture. I want to fuse the rational with the poetic. Architecture can be art, but that is not an end in itself. It's also social." Interview with Llàtzer Moix, published in *La Vanguardia,* 15 May 2005, Barcelona.

10. Ignasi de Solà-Morales: *Territorios,* Editorial Gustavo Gili, Barcelona, 2002.

The Barcelona Municipal Home for Seniors
2001–2005
Photographs by Lluís Casals

Following the festive excitement that the Forum left as its mark on the area, the eye-catching architectural displays and the rapid urban development required for the event, the time has come for a pause and a new awareness of the sense of the neighborhood. This is achieved by including activities, the residents and services for which a range of necessary infrastructure must, unsurprisingly, be built.

The health and socio-health center of the Municipal Healthcare Institute, built by the Clotet-Paricio duo, is the latest contribution in this sphere.

The building is part of a plan for an entire block at the junction between Avinguda Diagonal and Rambla Prim, very close to the Forum complex.

The site, which is somewhat larger than an Eixample block, is intended to hold the center and a considerable volume of offices with a surface area of more than 375,000 square feet that will have an important frontage overlooking the avenue. The buildings will gradually diminish in height towards the coast, giving rise to a construction on a more sensitive scale, the municipal home for seniors, and a square that will offer intriguing views.

The two buildings are united by their fractal geometry, which distinguishes their singular character as border posts in an intermediate area between the Forum constructions and the neighboring district. One of the intentions behind this geometry is to establish a reduction in height between the district and the newly-erected urban developments.

This axiom is the hallmark of the project, as the center straddles, as its architects recognize, "the new and the old," an experience that the architects of the successful remodeling of Boqueria Market were already familiar with.

The architects' approach is exceptional, as "the program for a home for seniors is very similar to that of a hotel in many respects, yet very different in others. Basically you sleep in a hotel, but you live in a home for the elderly. In a hotel, the rooms are important and the

corridors less so. Here the rooms are important, whereas the corridors are crucial. In a hotel, the relationship with the outdoor world can be reserved; here, it's good if the spectacle and life of the city can be seen from the inside."

The building itself is an angular volume generated by breaks that change on each floor and shape its outer appearance.

The double lines of facades are created using two different planes, one by way of a *brise-soleil* to provide protection against the sun, and the other to provide privacy as if it were the building's under garment. There is no connection between these planes and the distribution of the interior areas, as if they were apparently obeying different rules. The

outcome of this is the appearance of internal corridors that are architecturally very rich and which link the public and the private areas of the complex together.

Open-air or roofed interior courtyards are dotted around the perimeters, soaking up the space towards the exterior.

It is curious that a building of a markedly social nature should have a structure that more closely resembles a Baroque mansion than a health residence, in which the spacious and intense common areas and the well balanced distribution of the rooms assert themselves in an almost luxurious manner, for let us not forget that space is the highest manifestation of luxury in the 21st century.

In the words of the architects, "The project is intended to be an exercise in updating the old ideal of the Baroque facade, in which the public and the private do not deny any conflict but co-exist, do not disturb but rather enrich each other."

The Barcelona Botanical Gardens and Institute
1989–1999 / 2001–2003
Photographs by Alejo Bagué

The Botanical Gardens are one of the most attractive amenities that the city of Barcelona can offer residents. They are situated on the western slopes of Montjuïc Mountain as if turned away from the historic Olympic Stadium. The backdrop is provided by the Mediterranean Sea in one direction and the hills of Collserola in the other.

Triangulated concrete lines have been laid on this part of the mountain, following the lie of the land and forming a zigzagging network of paths that make their way up and down through the nearly 35 acres of the gardens. The routes thus fashioned serve to connect the various buildings and other amenities in the entire complex and also link the open spaces that act as natural squares offering services for the comfort and convenience of visitors.

The individual areas of the gardens are distributed between the paths in such a way as to organize the various collections of plants. The islands of land of varying size resulting from the crisscrossing of trails wending their way across the hill slope, the arrangement of the green expanses, the combination of rich hues and the position of the buildings, in particular the Botanical Institute, amidst the gardens provide a vibrant lesson in the art of landscaping.

In order to heighten the dramatic effect of this singular natural setting, walls have been erected, once again in triangulated shape, and lined with Cor-Ten steel—a material which, as it oxidizes, takes on earthy hues and a velvety texture that it retains even with the passage of time—prefiguring the terraces and retaining walls in colors very close to those of pine bark.

The Botanical Institute stands somewhat remote in a privileged spot on the hilltop, looking out like a large belvedere over the gardens from its position on an artificially leveled area that has allowed a clearing to be created for the entrance.

A rhythmical sequence of concrete ribs supports the structure of the two-storey building and organizes the interior space into exhibition areas on the ground floor and

working and administrative areas on the first floor.

From its commanding vantage point with impressive views, the Institute seems to provide protection to the gardens, which when seen from above look markedly Cubist to the eye.

Forum Building
2000–2004
Photographs by Duccio Malagamba

An enormous area of blue magma trapped inside invisible, intangible walls of an apparently pure geometry gives form to the Forum Building by Jacques Herzog and Pierre de Meuron.

A large, deliberately geometrical mass with the forthrightness of an equilateral triangle appears to be suspended, levitating slightly above the surface of the floor that rises and falls. This is an extraordinarily poetic declaration of intent, one whose provenance or connections with our present-day reality are hard to determine.

It is as if this were not a real building but the product of the illusion of a sweet dream in which spaces dissolve into each other without

us ever reaching the end, in which it is only by traveling through them that we can explain them, and only by passing through them are we granted the strange perception of how a unique space can flow and be transformed.

This is liquid architecture that generates the strange impression of "absence that is present", like that perceived in a dream but one that is consciously real, in which the sole contextual referent is the lower edges of the triangular prism that mark the borders and cut the external environment.

It is also difficult to anticipate the light in this building. The blend of direct, filtered and reflected light produces changes in the spaces, which go from a pasty density to a surprising

lightness—an effect in which once again the path traveled is the means of interpretation. The roofs covered with mirrored and waffle-effect sheets of metal—which also resolve the exterior finishes of the faced walls and the irregular courtyards scattered around the building floor plan and which are also treated with different finishes, including the occasional window—between them give rise to such a varied range that the light almost seems to take on a texture.

The glazed surfaces and covered open-plan areas on the ground floor make the light very changeable, giving it different formulations that eventually converge on the same space, generating a Baroque lighting effect that

cannot be described but in which the repeated reflection predominates.

If we add to this the fact that the natural sky mingles with the mirrors on the false ceiling, bouncing off the walls and inner courtyards, and if we also consider the various openings cut through, we can begin to get an idea that comes close to explaining the luminous, almost magical treatment of the building.

In contrast, the light is neutralized on the facades outdoors. In addition to the remarkable ability to absorb the ultramarine blue that dominates the three faces of the volume, there is the roughness of the surface to which it has been applied. This is a surface that retains the light before absorbing it like a sponge without allowing even the slightest trace of it to reflect. No gleam emanates from the facade, which greedily devours all the light that hits it.

The very different ways in which the interior and the exterior of this construction are worked are so extraordinarily opposed that they seem to be two different designs for the same building and arouse a disturbing sense of oneiric disorder. The effect is to make this a fascinating edifice.

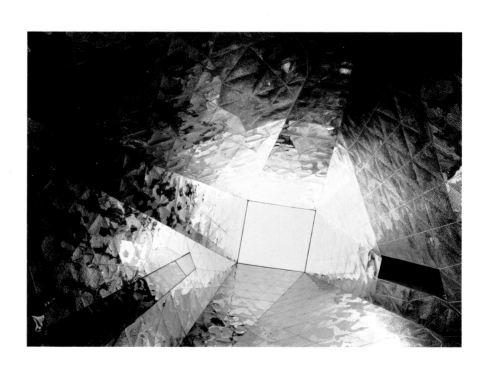

Josep Llinàs

Fort Pienc Complex
2001–2003
Photographs by Lurdes Jansana

In addition to the buildings erected in the important settings in the city such as Diagonal Mar, the Forum complex, Montjuïc, the new trade fair complexes and the area of Plaça de les Glòries, there are other projects that have perhaps not had the same media coverage but which have nevertheless structured high quality works in the heart of the city. These are less eye-catching, smaller undertakings but even so they wield tremendous influence in the areas where they are located.

The social services complex of Fort Pienc is one of the socially most sensitive projects so far this century in Barcelona, which has seen the construction of mammoth proposals, some of them veritable landmarks of modernity.

Fort Pienc is an architectural work erected in a neighborhood environment in an area of the Eixample that is in need of custom adaptations to enable it to cope with the pre-existing Ribes highway and the former El Norte train station, now used for buses, that linked the old quarter in the center of Barcelona with the urban nucleus of Horta.

Josep Llinàs' work for Fort Pienc is a solution in the form of a knot: a knot that pulls together this fragmented island in the Eixample and moors it to the old intercity highway; a knot that connects different functions with a strong personality of their own and which are a long way from each

other; a knot that binds different open, half-open and/or closed spaces.

The complex is organized as a macro volume with its main faces the facades on Carrer Sardenya and Carrer Alí Bei. It gradually breaks up towards the inner courtyard of the block till it reaches the square created from the extension of the old Ribes highway, which in turn acts as an epicenter. It is as if the entire construction were part of a quarry in which huge blocks of stone had fallen inwards.

The result is that of the three facades now in existence (the fourth, a primary school, is still under construction), the one corresponding to the square is especially attractive.

This facade is disjointed and has no clear

plane to indicate its situation. Instead, it is generated by the plural and structured meeting of the volumes that proceed either from the various parts of the architectural program or which are due to the impact of the structural elements of the construction.

It is a "non-facade" that forces the appearance of a large number of interesting corners, engendering mini-spaces of great architectural interest that emerge from seemingly chance moments and which have been charged with a particular mission to fulfill, which may be to spawn a part of the basement floor, to create a place of repose, to be an outdoor reception area, an occasional waiting area, meeting place, etc.

The new square that has been created is the point of access to most of the elements in the program: the library, the crèche, a small market, the civic center and the day center and nursing home for seniors. The exception to this is the hall of residence for students, which provides a support for the center at the point where it meets Carrer Sardenya, which is also where its entrance is located.

This slightly radial composition, with its center in the square, is dimly reminiscent of the approaches taken to rural constructions, in which new buildings are put up as the need arises, gradually giving rise to an outdoor vestibule with accesses to the various zones leading off it.

The height of the entire complex is very comfortable in scale and can easily be grasped by citizens, thereby enhancing the social and collective purpose of the center.

The quality of Llinàs' work was recognized by the 2004 City of Barcelona Prize for Architecture.

**CCIB, The Barcelona International
Convention Center**
2000–2004
Photographs by Xavier Ribas

One of the buildings needed in order to host the Forum of Cultures was a vast congress center for the conferences and debates on the themes of the event that would be attended by large numbers of delegates.

The commission was awarded to Josep Lluís Mateo, an architect from Barcelona with a distinguished international career and a professor at the ETH in Zurich.

The building is part of a larger project that includes two adjoining blocks, as Mateo himself recognizes: "The CCIB is not a single building but a group of diverse objects and programs."

It is a vast construction, as demonstrated by its surface area of more than 161,000 square feet, significantly larger than a block in the Eixample, or the huge 262-foot span of its main room, just less than the length of a soccer pitch.

The south facade looks out towards the sea and has a large window with a wooden canopy that offers spectacular views.

Outside, the building looks like an enormous cardboard box that has been turned upside down and somewhat crushed and deformed by an imaginary weight. This gives rise to the appearance of a series of folds that in turn produce meandering lines and almost warped surfaces on the facades.

The result is that the building seems visually less heavy than an excessively showy volume might have been. A further factor contributing to this effect is the fact that the inverted box rests on a sunken, glass plinth that once again refines the compactness of the building. This is a falsely opaque element in that it is covered with multi-perforated plaques that act as an exoderm and which are occasionally rendered transparent when the sun shines on them.

The quadrangular floor plan is organized by means of strips that run parallel to each other and perpendicular to the seafront, an ineluctable influence of the arrangement of the metal structure.

These strips are cut by a transverse asymmetrical axis, thereby dividing the building into two distinctive parts: the internal

organization or administrative area and the area used by the public.

The vertical communication and service elements are situated on this axis. This is where the long escalators of monumental character inside the building are to be found.

The access facade, facing the Forum Building, is distinguished from the rest of the construction by the enormous pergola that protects the entrance, with its remarkable yellow sign overhead.

On this side of the building, the plinth effectively configures the facade as it changes in both scale and design and is dotted with numerous small round windows that invite the passer-by to peer inside.

It is worth visiting this vast building when it is at rest, when its operating constants are at a low level, when there are no activities taking place, because then it arouses a strange sensation as if it were a destitute, ignored plantigrade waiting for someone to deal with it, and at that moment a pleasing and very different personal relationship is established with this magnificent edifice.

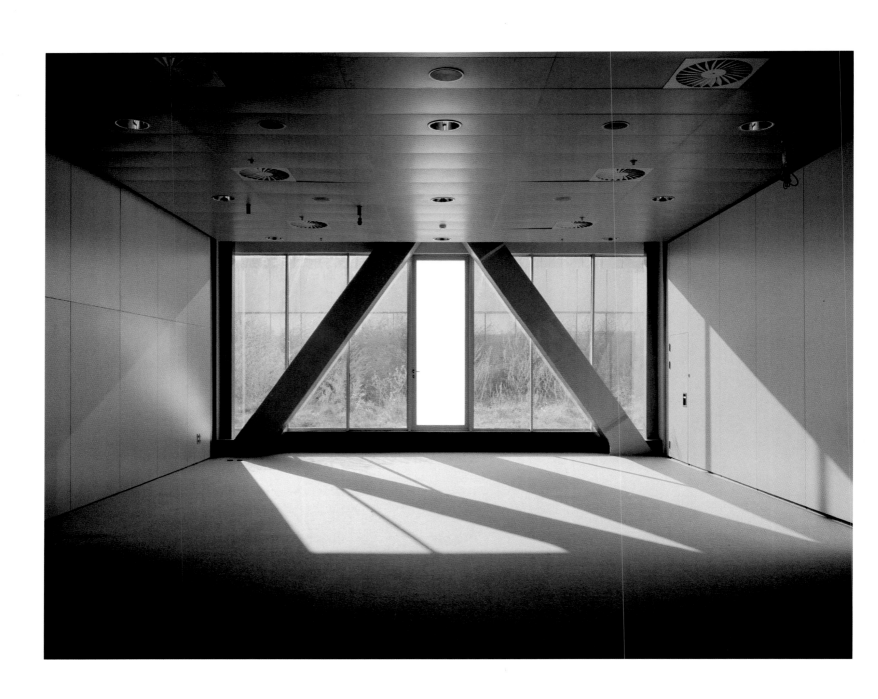

**MACBA, The Barcelona Museum of
Contemporary Art**
1987–1996
Photographs by Eugeni Pons

In 1969 Arthur Drexler organized an exhibition at the MoMA in New York entitled "The New York Five," in which he presented the five architects in the city that were to become leading figures in late modern and early postmodern architecture. These five architects were Michael Graves, Peter Eisenman, Charles Gwathmey, John Hejduk and Richard Meier.

The book that came out of this exhibition, *Five Architects,* published in 1972, became an international hit and a bestseller among the profession worldwide.

The exhibition was a launch pad, bringing to public attention American figures important enough to become part of highbrow architectural culture around the globe. Today,

all these architects, with the exception of Hejduk, who died in 2000, have built internationally renowned projects.

The career paths followed by the "five," the name they have been dubbed that will always identify them, have been as varied as their personal evolution, yet of them all, the constant rectitude of Meier's work is particularly striking.

Forty years of work have made him a great specialist in the design of museums, at which he excels.

Like the good "late modern" that he was, he began his career usefully in the offices of SOM and Marcel Breuer. In his works, Meier uses the dictionary of forms of the Modern

Movement, a dictionary that owes much of its content to the great master Le Corbusier, whom Meier acknowledges as a considerable influence on his work: the faces of the walls bathed in white; the sweeping glazed surfaces that quickly build the interior-exterior dialogue; the compositional importance of the vertical communication elements, often extended to the facade; the promenades; and the sly nod to the organic in the form of an undulating break at the most appropriate moments in the floor plan and/or the elevations.

The MACBA is one of Meier's exemplary works and a prime demonstration of his architecture, which remains loyal to the

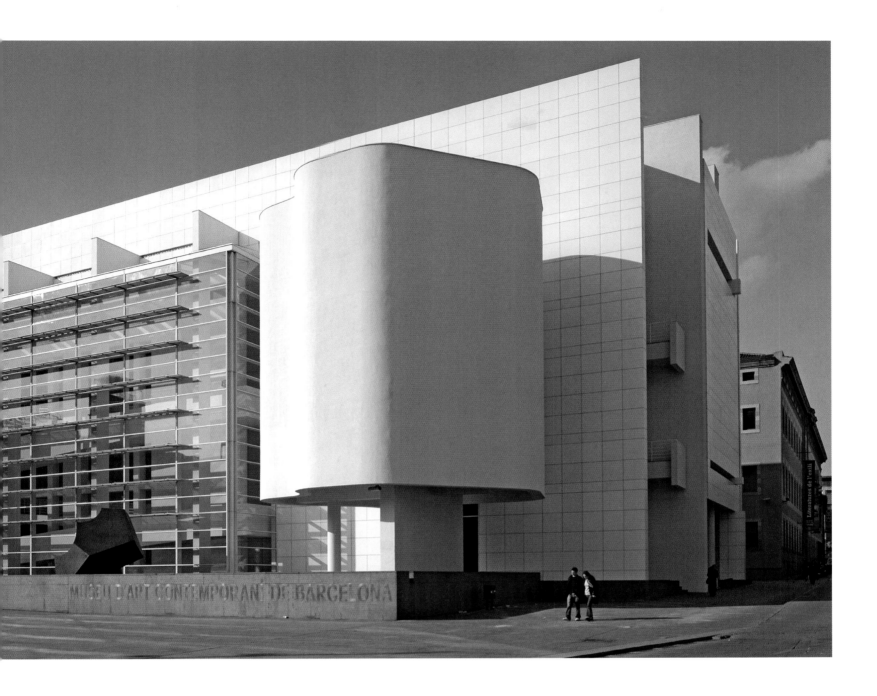

achievements and hallmarks of the Modern Movement, and which permits merely a flirtation with the use of new materials.

This is perhaps the finest possible building for this setting: it is a work that is oblivious to fashion, that has no local roots and that fits perfectly into its surroundings with surprising forthrightness.

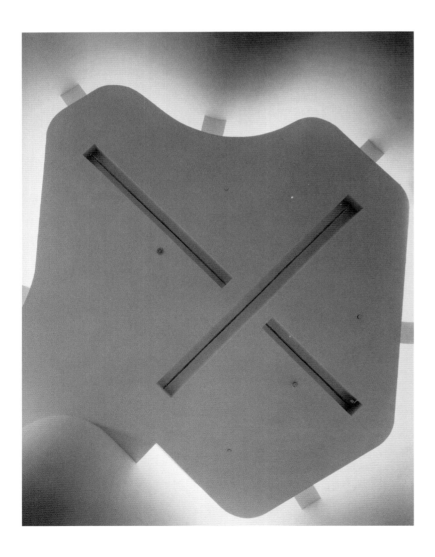

Santa Caterina Market
1997–2004
Photographs by Pepe Navarro

The roof of Santa Caterina Market is a rippling, continuous, multicolored cloak made up of hexagonal scales in a tremendous combination of greenish, purple, reddish and yellow hues that follow the curves of the folds of fabric.

This roof sweeps joyously beyond the surface marked out by the venerable perimeter walls and generously extends out over Avinguda Cambó and the rear of the market. This undulating, protective roof provides shelter for an ageing structure that the passing of the years has rendered in need of care.

This is an intense, elegant and gentle discourse. Even so, Miralles and Tagliabue's project goes beyond it to involve itself in time, and like time has gradually deposited layers on the place. Thus the location, which remains unchanged, may take new directions yet the things that once took place here remain an evident part of its present. The architects' design demonstrates a respect for earlier events—some long forgotten with the passing of the years and others already rediscovered and restored to memory—as if each season had left a fine patina behind it, year after year, so that in the end the place could not be understood without them.

And now that we have reached this point, there is yet more. Powerful structures growing with an organic care appear amid the internal elements with a naturalness that calls to mind the images of the Bomarzo Gardens, rising supremely upwards to form a swathe of steel and wood jungle and, with their complexity, unifying the edifice floating above the market stalls and the people.

Parts of the previous building have been integrated into the project and a symbiotic relationship has been forged between the old and the new, which has adapted to the original walls of the facades with their arcades, to which new untreated woodwork has been added with a barefaced naturalness, as if they had rushed headlong into a discourse so dense that it is capable of accepting or perhaps even of swallowing up a

new construction of something so distorting to itself as a home for seniors, radically transforming the language and making the work solidly and respectfully tectonic without altering the materials of the project.

This is a work steeped in Baroque organicism and executed using the simple and engagingly combined elements of steel, wood and concrete.

Back out on the street, the exuberant colors of the ceramic tiles of the roof astonish us with their joy and vitality, while at the back, a glass case displays the remains of the ancient ruins and reminds visitors of the historical background to the place.

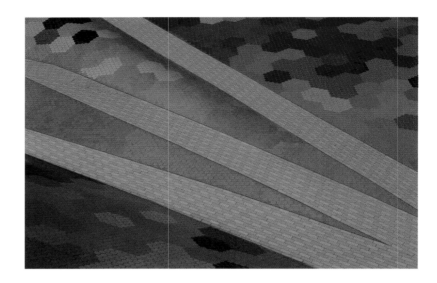

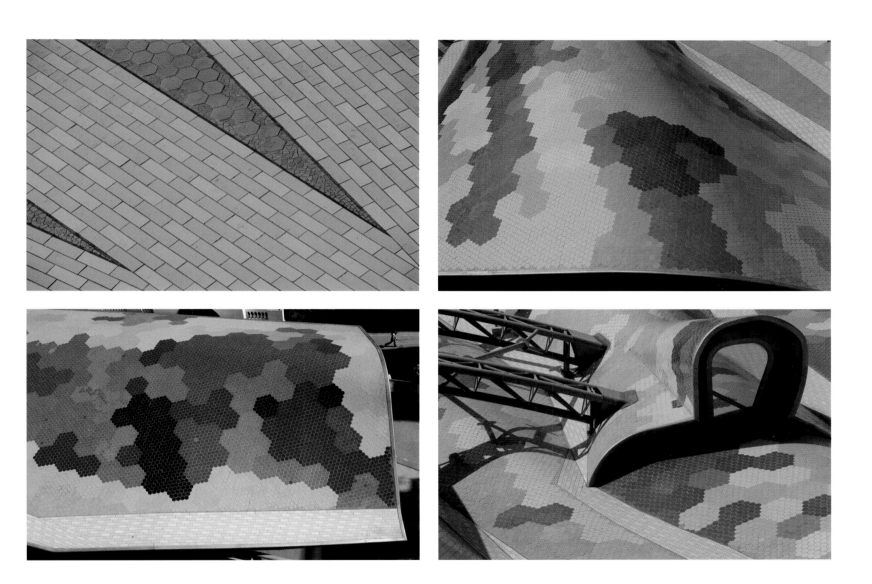

Barcelona Auditorium
1988–1994
Photographs by Hisao Suzuki

Rafael Moneo's work is characterized by the way his buildings stand magnificently in the location where they are constructed.

In his approach to his projects, Moneo devises a working methodology that judiciously combines a wealth of architectural culture with the skill of a great professional. Each building is like a manifesto or tribute to the history of architecture. As a result, each of his constructions is different to the others.

Consequently, if you cast your eye superficially over his buildings, you might think that his body of work is disjointed, yet an attentive consideration reveals historical and artistic references that make each project a historical novel in which the main character is the commission.

The Auditori is a case apart, as the architect himself recognizes: "on this occasion, the dialogue between the place and the architecture was going to be restricted unfortunately to a monologue," an unavoidable autonomy, which is really all that one means when one talks of a monologue.

The site is on Plaça de les Arts, a square that is home to a wealth of culture in the form of two major institutions, the Teatre Nacional and the Auditori, and which is formed as a result of a large fold in the Eixample near Plaça de les Glòries.

The project encompasses a vast program that includes the symphonic concert hall, a chamber music hall and the Catalan School of Music. The Music Museum, which is due to open in 2006, will add the finishing touch by incorporating services such as a library and workshop rooms, recording rooms, restaurants and stores.

Moneo has responded to the complexity of this project with a systematic sobriety that at first sight may seem excessively rigid. This rigidity is visible in the exterior of the building, as the sole license the architect has allowed himself is to build a large pedestal that gives the edifice an air of solemnity.

The exterior hardness of the building—in its floor plan and its facades—grants no

concessions to organics, instead pitting itself
against the extraordinary softness of the American
maple wood used extensively in the treatment
of the interiors, in which vigorous lines
predominate like rows of batons beating out the
rhythm of the volumes that shape the halls.

Just like a good symphony, the Auditori is a
piece with contained, exhaustive and intense
rigor. Or to use one of the most frequent
words in Moneo's vocabulary, it is a "lovely"
work.

Moneo works in the same way as an
orchestra conductor, carefully selecting the
piece to be played in each hall, performing it
in a free version and achieving an outstanding,
cultured and elegant innovativeness.

Agbar Tower
1999–2004
Photographs by Rafael Vargas

The Agbar Tower, to give the bare facts, has a constructed surface area of more than half a million square feet and reaches a lofty 500 feet or so in height.

This is not, however, the largest construction in the city, nor its tallest or most exuberant, but it is strikingly eye-catching. As is to be expected, it has been the subject of all kinds of comment. First came those who compared the building with a varied range of objects. Well-intentioned observations and smutty remarks, facile jokes and whimsical descriptions all spread rapidly by word of mouth.

Then came the short treatises which took the cultural approach, establishing links between the tower and skyscrapers and outlining their history and a giving lazy analysis of the rise of this type of building on the international scene at the present time, a discourse that had to be abandoned due to the limited stature—if you'll pardon the joke—of the leading character in the dramatis personae. Next came the formal coincidences, with comments on the similarities with the Swiss Re Tower, designed by Norman Foster's firm and recently erected in London, and another building, the Doha Tower, also by Nouvel, in Qatar, a spindle reaching the lofty height of more than 750 feet that is now at a very advanced stage of construction and which will provide us with the fascinating opportunity to observe how the surroundings manage to cope with a building of this nature.

At the same time, other mystical positions have emerged in which, if you will allow me a second joke, a certain levity has been employed in talking about light and the changing colors of the surface when it catches the sun, something that peaked with the completion of the lighting devices on the facade designed by Nouvel in collaboration with the sculptor Yann Kersalé that have 16 million possible combinations, promising us impressive spectacles of the kind seen hitherto only in Nevada.

The architectural and urban development viewpoint also made itself heard when it was

revealed, by chance, that the building enjoyed the company of other good-looking edifices that shared the limelight with it in the area.

Nor has the titillating accounting and financial factor been ignored, as we have been reminded that nearly 900,000 cubic feet of concrete and 250 tons of iron were used to build the tower, that it has 4,400 windows and that it is faced with 25,000 sheets of glass and has 4,500 lighting devices distributed across its facade. In addition, more than a thousand laborers and $155 million were required to build it.

All these different points of view and all this information build a nebulous image of one of the most significant buildings in Barcelona today, a special icon, as is evident to all, that will remain a presence in the city of tomorrow.

The Agbar Tower is a gently rotund building. Residents have quickly grown used to its rounded forms and the sight of it from various points around the city is always a pleasant surprise.

It should also be said that this is a changing building: its spectacular presence, when viewed from afar, gradually becomes more manageable the closer one gets to it, to the extent that at its foot it is agreeably domestic. The elements that the observer enters into contact with contribute to this effect and include a restrained entrance door, a pergola that is entirely appropriate and an eccentric perimeter fosse of very reasonable size. As you look upwards, the building's scaly skin made up of sheets of glass gradually merges into the sky, making it impossible to grasp the true height of the tower.

This is a new landmark for the city. And far from engaging in competition, it reveals a respect and admiration for the city's past and has become part of the history of the architecture of Barcelona.

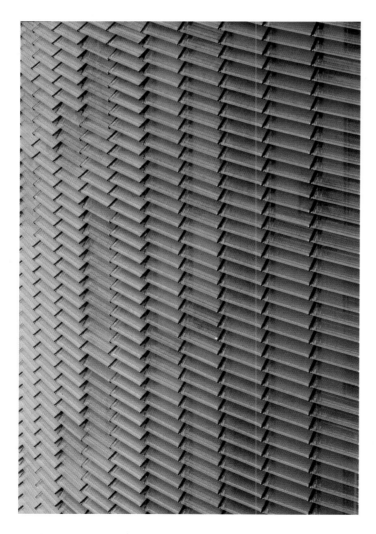

Location

p. 10

The Barcelona Municipal Home for Seniors
Lluís Clotet & Ignasi Paricio

2001–2005

Prim / Llull / Alfons el Magnànim / Taulat / Av. Diagonal

▶ Ⓜ L 4 (Maresme-Fòrum)
🚌 L 7, 41, 43, B23

The form of the buildings comply with the directrices of Cerdà's Eixample and Avinguda Diagonal, thereby fostering continuity between the scale of the Forum buildings and the consolidated urban tissue of the district, thanks to its uneven ground plan and different heights. According to the architects, the complex respects the tradition of tall Barcelona towers that rather than standing independently emerge from an uninterrupted mass of buildings that guarantees continuity and an attractive pedestrian itinerary.

p. 22

The Barcelona Botanical Gardens and Institute

Carles Ferrater

1989–1999 / 2001–2003

Jardí Botànic

▶ 🚌 L 55, 193

p. 34

Forum Building

Jacques Herzog & Pierre de Meuron

2001–2004

Av. Diagonal / Rbla. Prim

▶ Ⓜ L 4 (Maresme-Fòrum)
    🚌 L 7, 41, 43, B23

The Botanical Gardens—covering some 15 ha—stand on the northern slope of Montjuïc, forming a great south-east facing amphitheatre. The fundamental structure is a three-dimensional triangular mesh which adapts both to the terrain and to the different needs involved in the construction of the gardens: a variety of orientations, minimal earthworks, the creation of microclimates, the system of itineraries, irrigation, etc.

The Palau de Congressos was the venue for the Forum 2004 dialogues. The building is on two levels: the ground floor is a meeting place, a plaza open to public events. The floor above accommodates the concert hall, exhibition areas, congress rooms, restaurants and vestibules, all on the same level, which allows for maximum flexibility. A series of patios transfixes both levels, setting up different relationships between them and the light and water that cover the roof.

p. 50

Fort Pienc Complex

Josep Llinàs

2001–2003

Ausiàs March / Alí Bei / Sardenya / Sicília

▶ Ⓜ L 1 (Arc de Triomf)
🚌 L 6, 10, 19, 51, 54, 55, B25

"Almost a habitable sculpture" that exploits "violence and artifice" in response to irregular geometry—untypical of the Eixample—a varied program and diverse typologies: a market, a geriatric home, library, civic center and crèche. All the buildings open onto Carrer Ribes, which opens out into a plaza, the true scenario of the relationships between the different scales and volumes.

p. 62

CCIB, The Barcelona International Convention Center

Josep Lluís Mateo

2000–2004

Taulat / Rbla. Prim

▶ Ⓜ L 4 (Maresme-Fòrum)
🚌 L 7, 41, 43, B23

The CCIB is a complex of buildings that respond to a variety of functions, programs and clients. The hotel and the office block are arranged along Carrer del Taulat and structured in superimposed strips cut at a height of 164 feet above ground level. The convention center, for its part, stretches beneath a colossal metallic structure that, in the words of the architect, "complements the elegant neighbouring triangle". An undulating facade conceals the services area and provides the complex with a base.

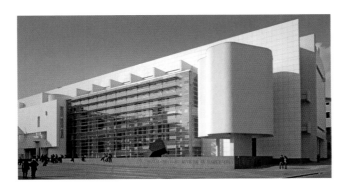

p. 76

MACBA, The Barcelona Museum of Contemporary Art

Richard Meier

1987–1996

Plaça dels Àngels, 1

▶ Ⓜ L 2 (Universitat), 3 (Catalunya)
   🚌 L 14, 59, 91, 120

p. 90

Santa Caterina Market

Enric Miralles & Benedetta Tagliabue

1997–2004

Av. de Francesc Cambó

▶ Ⓜ L 4 (Jaume I)
   🚌 L 17, 19, 40, 45

The building is accessed from the Plaça dels Àngels by means of a ramp that connects with the ground floor. Once inside, visitors continue along an inner ramp, located in the great three-storey atrium, which leads to the two floors above. This atrium is a point of reference and the protagonist of the building's image.

The rehabilitation of Santa Caterina Market modified former parameters of intervention in the old city to adapt to the complex qualities of the site. The project sets out to combine the construction of an underground car park, several buildings accommodating services and housing and the municipal market with archeological remains and the old market facades. Thus "the superimposition of different moments in time creates a spectacle of possibilities, creating the scenario for an interplay of variations".

p. 104

Barcelona Auditorium

Rafael Moneo

1988–1994

Lepant, 150

▶ Ⓜ L 1 (Marina)

🚌 L 6, 10

The building adopts the form of a single container, accommodating two concert halls with seating capacities for 2,500 and 700 people respectively, separated by a public foyer, a kind of open plaza dominated by a lantern-impluvium. A concrete gridiron clad with steel panels on the outside and oak panels on the inside envelops the entire building in a geometrical composition.

p. 116

Agbar Tower

Jean Nouvel

1999–2004

Plaça de les Glòries

▶ Ⓜ L 1 (Glòries)

🚌 L 7, 56, 92, B21

The tower, commissioned by the Barcelona Water Board, stands to one side of Plaça de les Glòries. The circular ground plan of the base is gradually reduced upwards towards the dome that crowns the building. The tower consists of two concrete walls: an interior nucleus containing the vertical communication nodes and the services, and the exterior wall that forms part of the facade. The floor-ceiling structures of the storeys are hung freely between one and the other. The different perforations in the exterior wall provide space for the windows, which support a second skin of glass slats.